Gerry the Seagull was always searching for food,
but one day he saw something totally new.
This "Octo's Tacos," looked like something to eat
He swooped down to check it out
hoping it was sweet.
But when he met Octo,
Octo was sad.
So far everyone had thought
that new
equaled bad.

Octo explained his magical food;
for a taco could be made for any mood.
"Gerry, I can make you a taco that's sweet,
or one with no cheese, no meat & no wheat."
Gerry said, "I would love to try something new,
and hopefully help you not feel so blue."
...and?
He loved it!
"Wow Octo, that Octo's Taco was truly the best,
now I can't wait to try all the rest!"

Gerry was so excited about his new discovery.
His dreams that night
made the moon & starfish hungry.
By morning he had a plan for everyone to try them.
He knew to love Octo's Tacos
they just had to have some.
He decided to play a big show for the whole town
and sing a song about tacos
to get rid of Octo's frown.
Now, he just needed to form his new band.
He started with his neighbors
who live close to the sand.

Gerry flew up to see Salty Raven first
and brought a fresh taco up to his perch.
"Salty Raven, you put the BANG
in the BING BANG BOOM!
I need your drums for my band,
or Octo's Tacos is DOOMED!"
"What's an Octos Tacos?
Is this a new kind of cymbal or drum?
It looks like I would just break it
and we both would be bummed ..."

"You don't hit it like a cymbal or drum.
Octo's Tacos are food and super yum!
Once you try them
you'll want to BING BANG BOOM."
Salty Raven had just eaten,
but he could always make room.
And...?
He loved it!
"You were right Gerry,
Octo's Tacos are super delicious.
I'll join your band and
help fulfill Octo's wishes!"

Gerry brought a taco to Crabarita.
Her maracas playing is muy bonita!
"Crabarita, I need your beautiful sound
to help me turn Octo's Tacos around!"
"What's an Octos Tacos?"
Is this a surf board?
It's as big as my head.
I'm afraid it'll break up
as soon as it's wet!"

"You don't ride a taco into the ocean.
You cover it in one of Octo's potions.
He calls them salsas, they're simply amazing.
Once you try one it's all you'll be craving!"
Crabarita looked at the huge food in her claw
and took the littlest bite you ever saw.
...and?
She loved it!
"I've never tasted anything so delicious!
I guess I needn't be so suspicious..."

Then to the lighthouse Gerry did fly
for that's where the best keytar player ever resides
"Tuskadero Slim,
please take a break from watching the sea,
and play for my band your sweet melody!"
Gerry presented Tuskedero with a taco
with extra seaweed.
"To save Octo's Tacos,
your keytar is what's needed!"
"What's an Octo's Tacos?
What sort of tiny boat did you collect?
If this hits the seas it's sure to be wrecked!"

"It's not a boat to ride to the shore,
It's a delicious food delivered right to your door
Octo made this taco especially for you.
If you join my band
everyone else can try them too!"
Tuskadero ate the taco
and decided it wasn't a boat.
In fact it was so tasty
he had to take note.
"I love it!
I'll help you with the melody-
this is delicious, I have to agree."

Gerry knew for his band to be truly great
he needed Mr Big on Bass!
It was worth flying deep into the forest
to get Mr Big for the band.
He's flawless!
"Mr Big, with your bass lines
we can Rock This Town:
Octo's Tacos all around!"
"What's an Octos Tacos?"
Mr Big looked at the taco.
"That mushroom might not be to consume.
If it's poisonous it would surely bring gloom..."

"It's not a "Fungi, Big Guy!
It's the tastiest food
you'll ever try!
Join my band and leave your huge nest
there's no Octo's Tacos in this forest."
Mr Big loved food, so he didn't gripe
he ate the whole taco
in just one bite, and...?
He loved it!
"Wow Gerry, I could eat 100 of those!
and I can't wait to make sure
everyone knows!"

DJ LlamaRama spins the
sweetest mixes and the freshest beats!
She gets everyone moving up on their feet.
Gerry brought her a taco
at her dance beach party
and danced with friends
Coco, Lemmy, and Shorty.
"DJ LlamaRama you can make anyone dance!
Help me give Octo's Tacos a chance!"
"What's an Octos Tacos?
Is that album bent?" she said with a grin.
"Gerry, now that vinyl will never spin..."

"It's yummy food to eat,
not a way to spin a beat!
With you in the band
everyone will be dancing.
Once you try Octo's Tacos
you're sure to be prancing!"
DJ LlamaRama wasn't so sure about
trying something new,
but after a minute she decided to,
and ...?
She loved it!
"I'll mix a beat so fly
this whole town will come by!"

Gerry's band wrote their song and threw a big show
and told their friends, "Invite everyone you know
At Octo's food truck they sang the taco song
to a huge crowd who soon sang along...

"So you never heard of Tacos? Well that's just swe
Tacos are your favorite foods in a tortilla shell.
You can eat them for breakfast with eggs and ham
or have them for lunch with fish in them.
Whatever filling you decide to choose
with Octo's Tacos you just can't lose!
Tacos, tacos, tacos are good to eat
Tacos, tacos, tacos are such a treat!"

After the show
and for the days that followed,
The wind carried the story
to those deep and shallow.
Soon Octo's Tacos was the place to be
and on most days
a line could be seen.
Now that Octo's Tacos was a popular spot,
Octo had the time to rock!
He busted out his custom two headed guitar,
and joined Gerry's band
for shows near and far.

THE END

Dedicated to the Real Gerry the Seagull
& his home of Tillamook, OR.

For more Flock of Gerrys go to:
www.flockofgerrys.com